3 1257 01865 4219

Schaumburg Township District Library
130 South Roselle Road
Schaumburg, Illinois 60193

Schaumburg Township District Library
130 South Roselle Road
Schaumburg, IL 60193
847-985-4000
For Renewals:
schaumburglibrary.org
847-923-3158

Good Manners in Public

Excuse me...

by Katie Marsico
illustrated by John Haslam
Content consultant: Robin Gaines Lanzi, PhD, MPH,
Department of Human Science, Georgetown University

magic
wagon

SCHAUMBURG TOWNSHIP DISTRICT LIBRARY
JUVENILE DEPT.
130 SOUTH ROSELLE ROAD
SCHAUMBURG, ILLINOIS 60193

409
ABDO

395.5
MARSICO, K

3 1257 01865 4219

visit us at www.abdopublishing.com

Published by Magic Wagon, a division of the ABDO Group, 8000 West 78th Street, Edina, Minnesota, 55439. Copyright © 2009 by Abdo Consulting Group, Inc. International copyrights reserved in all countries. All rights reserved. No part of this book may be reproduced in any form without written permission from the publisher.

Looking Glass Library™ is a trademark and logo of Magic Wagon.

Printed in the United States.

Text by Katie Marsico
Illustrations by John Haslam
Edited by Amy Van Zee
Interior layout and design by Becky Daum
Cover design by Becky Daum

Library of Congress Cataloging-in-Publication Data
Marsico, Katie, 1980-
  Good manners in public / by Katie Marsico ; illustrated by John Haslam.
     p. cm. — (Good manners matter!)
  Includes bibliographical references (p.   ).
  ISBN 978-1-60270-610-1
  1. Etiquette for children and teenagers. 2. Public spaces—Juvenile literature. I. Haslam, John. II. Title.
  BJ1857.C5M1267 2009
  395.5'3—dc22

                    2008036322

Contents

Why Do Good Manners Matter in Public?

Achoo! You sneeze as you walk down the street. Having a cold is no fun! What can you do about that sneezing though? Is it all right to sneeze on everyone around you? You may have been in this situation in public before. How did you handle yourself?

Going out in public is a great time to practice thinking of others. If you are unsure how to act, ask a grown-up for advice!

Picture what going out in public would be like if no one had good manners. People might be loud at places like the library where they should be quiet. They might push each other in line at the store. Everyone would cough and sneeze on each other.

You would never want to go anywhere if people were this rude. But life would be pretty boring if you never left your house. This is why it's important to have good manners in public. Let's think about how you can show good manners in public.

Using good manners will make you fun to be around. Others will want to spend time with you if you show them that you care about them.

Show Good Manners in Public!

Where do you go out in public? Public places you visit might include libraries, restaurants, and parks. Being in public often means being around lots of other people. Remember to treat them with respect. Showing respect lets others know that you care about them.

Different places require different manners. It is all right to shout and run at the park. But that would be bad manners at the library. Be aware of where you are and those around you!

One way to show respect is to practice good manners. You can practice good manners no matter where you go. Cover your mouth and nose when you sneeze or cough. It is also polite to say "bless you" when other people sneeze. This is a nice way to tell them you hope they feel better soon.

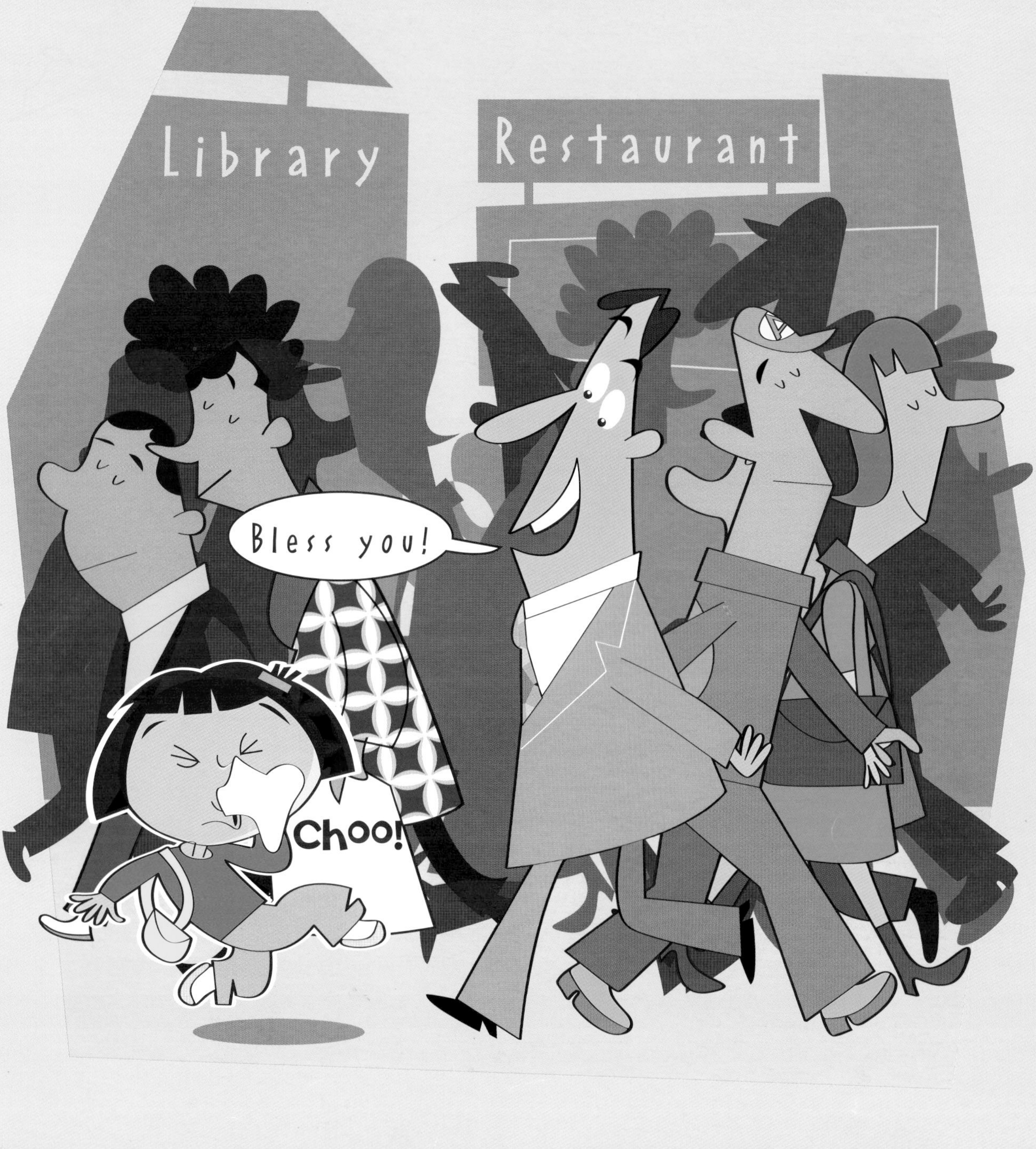
Library
Restaurant
Bless you!
Choo!

Another example of good manners is to hold the door open for the people behind you. And at the grocery store, remember to respect your parents. Don't complain or yell if you don't get something you want.

Just like at school or on the playground, always wait your turn in lines. Pushing will not make the line go any faster!

Remember to respect the grown-ups who work at public places. Follow any rules they explain to you. For example, the lifeguard at the pool may tell you about rules you must follow in the water. The crossing guard tells you when to stay on the sidewalk. Then, he or she lets you know when it's safe to cross the street.

Practicing good manners in public will help you stay safe. Good manners will also help you and those around you have more fun!

It is also good to be polite when you greet people. When you see someone you know, say "Hi! How are you?" If you see someone who looks or acts different than you, don't stare or point. Do your best to make that person feel welcome. These are all examples of great manners!

Be polite to new kids you meet. You could say, "Hi. My name is Charlie. Do you want to play?"

There are some words that show you have good manners anywhere you are. Saying "thank you," "you are welcome," "excuse me," and "please" are polite no matter where you go. Let's get ready to see some good manners in motion!

Manners in Motion

Ben headed to the library for story time. He was excited to see his friends when he walked in the door. He couldn't wait to join them in the circle around the librarian! Ben knew it would be rude to shout "hi" at them from across the room. Lots of people were trying to read their books. They would be bothered by the noise.

"Hello, everyone! How are all of you doing today?" Ben asked quietly when he got closer.

"I'm great, Ben," answered Lisa. "Would you like to sit next to me?" Lisa moved over to make a spot for him.

"Thank you," answered Ben.

Soon the librarian began story time. The librarian asked everyone to stay quiet until she was done reading. Then they could all talk about the book.

When story time was over, Ben and Lisa decided to check out some books. The two friends stood in line at the desk. Lisa was ahead of Ben. The line to check out books was long. They didn't mind though. It was a chance for them to talk quietly.

"How are you feeling, Ben?" Lisa asked. Ben was getting over a cold.

"I'm much better," Ben answered. "Thanks for asking, Lisa." Then, Ben felt like he was about to sneeze. He quickly covered his mouth and nose. "*Achoo!* At least I thought I was much better!"

"Bless you," said Lisa. "I bet your cold will be gone soon. Please go ahead of me. You should get home and curl up in bed with a good book!"

Can you name all the different ways Ben and Lisa practiced good manners in public? Having good manners is easy! Just remember to be polite and show respect for the people around you. What good manners have you practiced in public lately?

Amazing Facts about Manners in Public

Did Someone Sneeze?

What should you say if you hear someone sneeze in India? In the United States, you say "bless you" when someone sneezes. But not everyone says the same thing! In India, you would say "live well!" People in Russia answer children's sneezes with the words "be healthy and grow big!" These sayings are all examples of good manners.

Hands Out of Your Pockets Please!

Have you ever walked down the street with your hands in your pockets? You probably wouldn't do this if you lived in Mexico! People there think it is bad manners to do this in public.

Top Five Tips for Good Manners in Public

1. Cover your mouth if you cough or sneeze.
2. Greet others by saying "hi!"
3. Don't be loud in a quiet place, such as the library.
4. Wait your turn in line.
5. Don't forget to say "please," "thank you," and "excuse me!"

Glossary

crossing guard—someone who helps people cross the street.
greet—saying something friendly when you meet or see someone.
lifeguard—a worker who protects swimmers.
polite—showing good manners by the way you act or speak.
respect—a sign that you care about people or things and want to treat them well.
rude—showing bad manners by the way you act or speak.
situation—the event of a certain moment.

Web Sites

To learn more about manners, visit ABDO Group online at **www.abdopublishing.com**. Web sites about manners are featured on our Book Links page. These links are routinely monitored and updated to provide the most current information available.

Index